HAPPY VALENTI DAY!

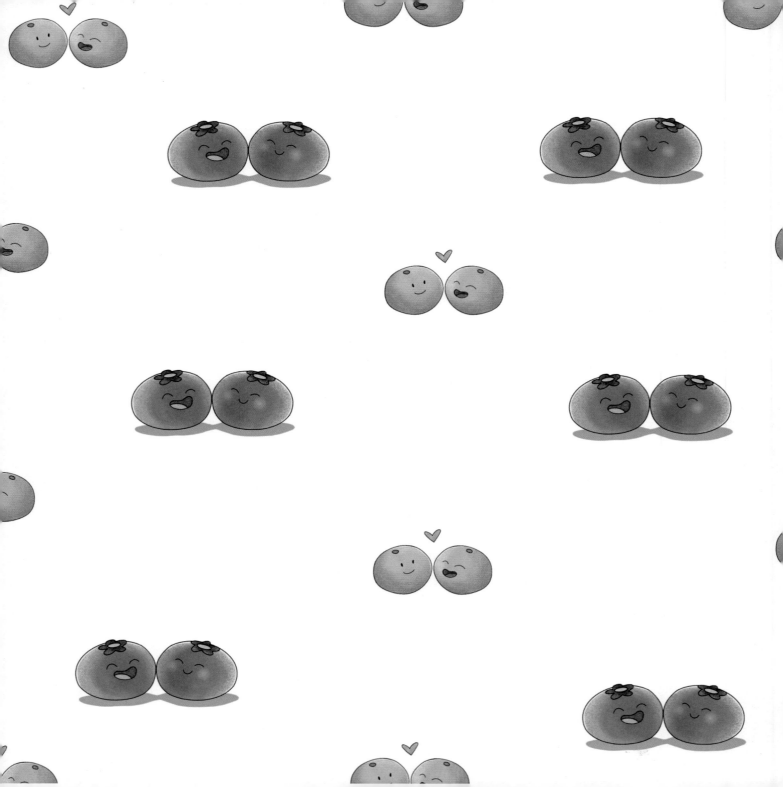

Q. What did the boy octopus say to the girl octopus?

A. "I want to hold your hand, hand, hand, hand, hand, hand, hand, hand."

Are you a triangle?

Because you sure are acute!

Q. Why did the frog cross the road?

A. Because he wanted to show his girlfriend he had guts.

Q. What happened to the bed bugs who fell in love?

A. They got married in the spring.

Q. What did one raspberry say to the other on Valentine's Day?

A. "I love you berry much."

Q. What do ghosts say to one another to show that they care?

A. "I love BOO!"

Q. What do bunnies do when they get married?

A. Go on a bunnymoon!

Q. What did the paper clip say to the magnet?

A. "I find you very attractive."

Q. Do skunks celebrate Valentine's Day?

A. Yes, they're very scent-imental!

Q. What did the bat say to his girlfriend?

A. You're fun to hang around with.

Q. What did the lightbulb say to his girlfriend?

A. "I love you a whole watt!"

Q. What do you call the world's smallest Valentine's Day card?

A. A Valen-teeny!

Q. What did the slug say to her boyfriend on Valentine's Day?

A. "Will you be my Valen-slime?"

Knock, knock

Who's there?

Olive

Olive who?

Olive you.

Q: What did the stamp say to the envelope?

A: I'm stuck on you.

Q: What did the squirrel give for Valentine's Day?

A: Forget-me-nuts

Q: What did the farmer give his wife for Valentine's Day?

A: Hogs and kisses

Q: What did one volcano say to the other volcano

A: I lava you!

Q: What did the calculator say to the pencil on Valentine's Day?

A: You can always count on me.

Q: What did the blueberry say to his wife on Valentine's Day?

A: I love you berry berry much.

Q: Where do cows go on a Valentines date?

A: To the moo-vies!

Q: How do you ask a dinosaur to lunch?

A: Tea Rex?

Q: What did the elephant say to his girlfriend on Valentine's Day?

A: I love you a ton.

Q: What kind of valentines chocolate is never on time?

A: ChocoLATE

Q: What did the bear say to his wife?

A: Life without you would be unBEARable

Q: What did the drum say to her boyfriend?

A: My heart beats for you!

Q: What did one boat say to the other boat?

A: Are you interested in a little row-mance?

Q: What did one plate say to the other plate on Valentines?

A: Dinner is on me!

Knock, knock.
Who's there?
Iguana.
Iguana, who?
Iguana love you forever and always.

Q: What did the toilets wife do when he gave her a compliment?

A: She flushed.

Q: What did one avocado half say to the other?

A: "Without you, I'm empty inside!"

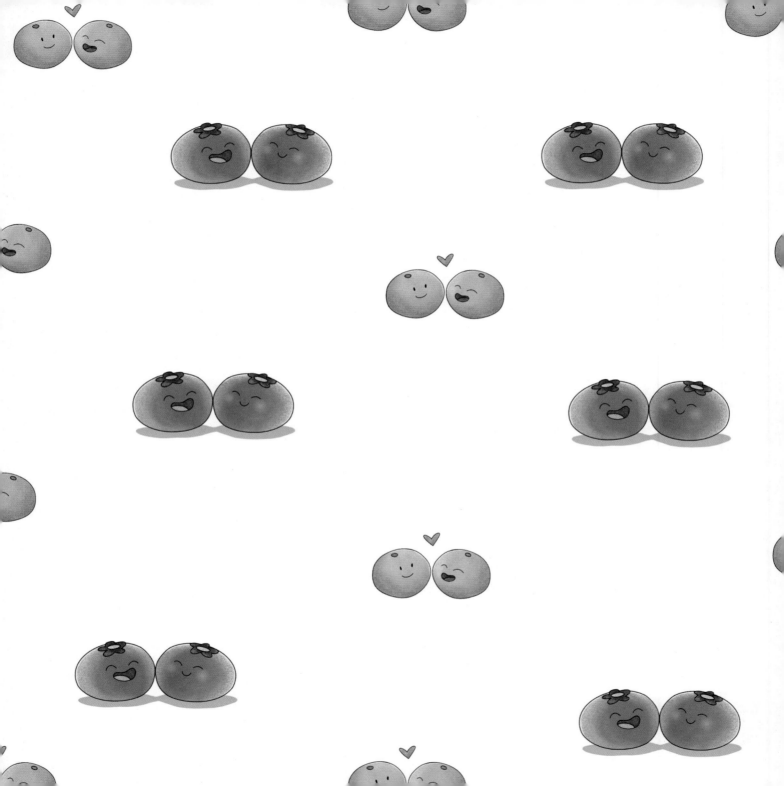

Made in the USA
Las Vegas, NV
16 February 2021

17907416R10024